Happy Birthday Whit —
A new decade to make yours
mark ... A mark that can change
lives.
Here's to a new adventure
that fills your life with love &
happiness. All Our Love,
Mom & Dad

2016

A GIFT FOR:

Whitney

FROM:

Love,
Mom & Dad

12/11/16

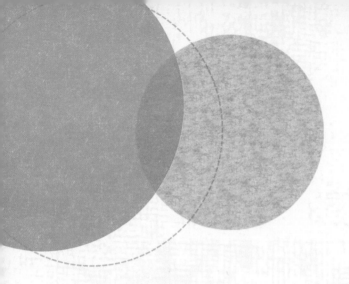

Art Director: Chris Opheim
Editor: Theresa Trinder
Designer: Laura Elsenraat
Production Designer: Dan Horton

Published by Hallmark Gift Books,
A division of Hallmark Cards, Inc.,
Kansas City, MO 64141
Visit us on the Web at Hallmark.com.

ISBN: 978-1-59530-782-8
1BOK2223
Made in China

NOW YOU'RE 30!

MILESTONES & MEMORIES FOR YOUR GENERATION

By Brandon M. Crose

> "ALL THAT I KNOW
> I LEARNED AFTER I WAS THIRTY."
> —*Georges Clemenceau*

You've been called Generation Y and—your favorite!—a "Millennial." You were a child of the nineties, when Clarissa explained it all, boy bands were big, and Alanis Morissette interpreted "ironic" a little differently than Merriam-Webster did. Older people seem to have a lot of opinions about so-called Millennials, but did they count September 11th as the last day of their childhood or have to land their first real job during the Great Recession? Maybe, just maybe, your technological expertise and penchant for "selfies" and photo filters isn't the whole story. The truth is, you have seen a lot in a little time... but your story has really just begun.

WHEN YOU WERE BORN...

IN THE NEWS

The Reagan administration found itself in hot water when an American cargo plane carrying weapons and military supplies intended for Contra guerrillas was shot down and its illegal purpose discovered.

Millions watched in horror as the space shuttle Challenger—whose crew included Christa McAuliffe, a school teacher—exploded moments after takeoff.

George H. W. Bush accepted his party's nomination at the Republican National Convention by making a pledge that would later haunt his presidency: "Read my lips—no new taxes."

Your parents might have had to do "duck and cover" drills in school, but you would not: the Cold War came to a symbolic end with the fall of the Berlin Wall.

The Exxon Valdez, piloted by an inexperienced third mate, went off course and struck a reef in Alaska's Prince William Sound, spreading over 11 million gallons of crude oil over 1,300 miles of pristine coastline.

WHEN YOU
WERE BORN

EVENTS

Most thought the AIDS epidemic was only a threat to some...until 13-year old Ryan White acquired the virus through a blood transfusion and fought courageously to educate the world that this deadly disease was a threat to all.

Maybe your parents purchased a new Cometron or Comet Catcher telescope to watch the passing of Halley's Comet? If you were too young to remember seeing the orbiting ball of ice and dust, don't worry— you'll have another chance in 2062!

The wreck of the RMS Titanic was at last found—broken in two and 12,000 feet under the North Atlantic. What your parents didn't know was that this discovery happened during a top-secret Navy mission to find the remains of two Cold War-era nuclear submarines.

Slain civil rights leader Martin Luther King, Jr. was honored with the dedication of a new national holiday, though, initially, only 27 states observed it.

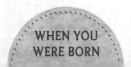

WHEN YOU
WERE BORN

"YOU KNOW THAT WE ARE
LIVING IN A MATERIAL WORLD
AND I AM A MATERIAL GIRL"

Madonna—*Material Girl*, 1984

MUSIC

You may not remember now, but "Everybody Wants to Rule the World" by Tears for Fears, "That's What Friends Are For" by Dionne and Friends, and "I Wanna Dance with Somebody (Who Loves Me)" by Whitney Houston were likely among the first songs you ever heard.

VH1 joined MTV to bring the world trend-setting music videos by '80s icons like Madonna, Michael Jackson, Cyndi Lauper, and Peter Gabriel.

Maybe your parents watched the broadcast of Live Aid (along with 1.9 billion other people all over the world). A benefit to relieve famine in Ethiopia, the American concert closed with USA for Africa's hit "We Are the World."

First featured in a commercial for the California Raisin Industry, four singing raisins spawned four albums, two TV specials, and a host of merchandise. The shriveled superstars are now part of the Smithsonian's permanent collection.

WHEN YOU
WERE BORN

NOW SHOWING:

TOP GUN

FERRIS BUELLER'S DAY OFF

BACK TO THE FUTURE

MOVIES

Blockbuster popcorn flicks reigned supreme: your parents may have seen *Back to the Future, Aliens,* and *Who Framed Roger Rabbit* in the theater. Several times.

Tom Cruise inspired a fashion throwback with *Top Gun*: leather bombers and aviator glasses. (And perhaps influenced more than just fashion—Navy enlistments skyrocketed after the hit film's release.)

Critical hits *She's Gotta Have It* and *Do the Right Thing* lifted young African-American director Spike Lee to prominence.

Many of John Hughes's films, including *The Breakfast Club, Pretty in Pink, and Ferris Bueller's Day Off,* are still classics today.

The big screen (and box office) stars included Eddie Murphy, Cher, Arnold Schwarzenegger, Glenn Close, Sylvester Stallone, Meryl Streep, Michael J. Fox, and Clint Eastwood.

WHEN YOU
WERE BORN

TV

Your parents grew up with only three to five channels, but now there were almost 60! By the time you were born, nearly half of all American homes had cable TV. (Though some, perhaps, came to agree with Bruce Springsteen: "There's 57 channels and nothing on!")

With so many more options, how could your parents possibly watch it all? VCRs to the rescue! Television executives wrung their hands in fear that their audience would simply fast forward through the commercials. (Which many did.)

Your parents' favorite shows may have included *Dallas*, *The Cosby Show*, *Cheers*, *Family Ties*, *Miami Vice*, or *Moonlighting*.

The new network Fox challenged CBS, NBC, and ABC for dominance by introducing a dysfunctional yet hilarious new family: *The Simpsons*, who became the most popular animated family on primetime since *The Flintstones*.

WHEN YOU
WERE BORN

Before his illegal betting got him ousted from baseball, Cincinnati Reds batter Pete Rose surpassed 4,191 hits to break a record set 57 years earlier by Ty Cobb.

If it hadn't yet, the widespread cocaine epidemic of the mid '80s likely got your parents' attention when it claimed two athletes: Len Bias, newly drafted by the Boston Celtics, and professional football player Don Rogers.

Whether your parents admired her for her speed or her singular fashion sense, Florence Griffith Joyner (or "FloJo") set records in the 100- and 200-meter dashes at the 1988 Summer Olympics in Seoul, Korea.

Because of the success of sports television, your parents might have started following some previously lesser-known sports, such as volleyball, water polo, wrestling, monster truck shows, and car racing.

WHEN YOU
WERE BORN

POP CULTURE

Perhaps you bear one of the most popular baby names of the decade: Michael, Christopher, Matthew, Joshua, or David. And for girls: Jessica, Ashley, Amanda, Jennifer, or Sarah.

Nintendo was born about the same time you were! "Mario" and "Zelda" became household names as the original Nintendo Entertainment System sold over 60 million units in its first two years.

The private lives of celebrities were suddenly matters of great interest. Supermarket tabloids—such as *Star, The Globe,* and *The National Enquirer*—sold by the tens of millions.

Minimum wage was $3.35, and the median household income was approximately $24,000. A single-family home may have cost your parents around $92,000. A promotion at work? Perhaps they financed a Hyundai for $4,995 or, if they had the means, a new Cadillac Brougham for $20,159.

WHEN YOU WERE BORN

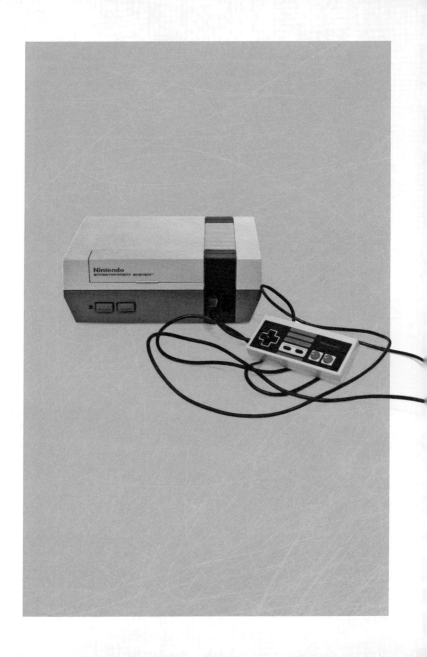

WHEN YOU WERE A KID...

IN THE NEWS

Still reeling from race riots after the Rodney King trial just two years earlier, Los Angeles was rocked by an early morning earthquake measuring 6.6 on the Richter Scale. It lasted only 40 seconds, but that was long enough to destroy several buildings and freeways, killing 55 people.

If your parents let you watch the news, the massive disaster of Oklahoma City bombing surely left quite an impression, and you may also remember when the Unabomber's manifesto appeared in the *New York Times* or the *Washington Post*—it was jointly printed in both papers.

In hopes of boarding a UFO they believed to be trailing the Hale–Bopp comet, thirty-nine members of the Heaven's Gate cult, led by Marshall Applewhite, committed mass suicide in a California mansion.

WHEN YOU
WERE A KID

The world was stunned when
Princess Diana and her boyfriend,
Dodi Al-Fayed, were killed
in a car accident while trying
to avoid the paparazzi.
Mother Teresa, a close friend
of the princess, died of natural
causes only five days later.

"You've got mail!" People were checking their e-mail, joining chat rooms, and browsing the Web on full-service programs like America Online, Prodigy, and CompuServe. If you were lucky, your parents may have even installed an extra phone line to "log on" without getting "booted" when the telephone rang.

Science was doing amazing things: lasers were approved to perform precise eye surgery, genetic modification allowed farmers to begin growing produce that was larger and more resistant to insecticides, and scientists in Scotland successfully cloned a lamb named Dolly, igniting a worldwide debate about the implications of cloning technology.

Advances in cancer treatment and breakthroughs in gene therapy meant not only that those living with sickness had a better chance of survival, but also that there was now an even better chance of prevention.

Continuous research in drugs suppressing the Human Immunodeficiency Virus (HIV), once considered a death sentence, led to more effective treatments—and longer lives.

WHEN YOU
WERE A KID

MUSIC

With their international hits "I'll Never Break Your Heart," "Quit Playing Games (with My Heart)," and "As Long as You Love Me," the Backstreet Boys ignited the "boy band" craze of the late '90s, with NSYNC and 98 Degrees quick to follow.

When radio was reluctant to play songs by female singer-songwriters, they got together and threw a concert. The Lilith Fair featured preeminent female musicians Sarah McLachlan, the Indigo Girls, Paula Cole, Fiona Apple, Sheryl Crow, Jewel, Natalie Merchant, and many others. The concert made $16 million over 38 shows.

Some of your other favorite songs might have included "Ironic" by Alanis Morissette, "Wannabe" by the Spice Girls, or "I Believe I Can Fly," by R. Kelly.

WHEN YOU
WERE A KID

Elton John rewrote an old song and performed it at the funeral of Princess Diana. "Candle in the Wind '97" quickly sold 34 million copies, and all proceeds were donated to charity.

MOVIES

The blockbuster movies of your childhood years may include *The Lion King*, *Toy Story*, *Clueless*, and *Independence Day*.

Forrest Gump introduced the philosophy "Life is like a box of chocolates," and Jim Carrey became the funny man of the decade with hit movies *Ace Ventura: Pet Detective*, *Dumb and Dumber*, and *Liar Liar* (for which he was paid $20 million).

Be honest: how many times did you watch that ship and iceberg collide? New computer technology allowed for special effects on a previously unimagined scale, and *Titanic* paved the way for future CGI spectacles.

"Movie night" didn't always mean going to the theater—all you had to do was rent a VHS tape from the local Blockbuster Video and pop it into your VCR. (Let's just hope you didn't forget to rewind!)

WHEN YOU
WERE A KID

TV

Your favorite shows may have included hits from the TGIF lineup: *Family Matters, Boy Meets World, Step by Step, Hangin' with Mr. Cooper,* and *Sabrina, the Teenage Witch.*

But your favorite cartoons were just as memorable: *Doug, Sailor Moon, The Magic School Bus, Aaahh!!! Real Monsters, Rocko's Modern Life, Teenage Mutant Ninja Turtles...*

Pop Up Video on VH1 was a big deal, and other, more "adult" shows you enjoyed (if your parents let you watch them) might have included *Star Trek: The Next Generation, Touched by an Angel,* and *Walker, Texas Ranger.*

You probably remember staying up late to watch the O. J. Simpson police chase. Every minute of the slow pursuit, and the subsequent eight-month trial (dubbed "The Trial of the Century" by a perhaps too-enthusiastic news media), was aired live and watched by millions.

WHEN YOU
WERE A KID

SPORTS

The 1996 Summer Olympics in Georgia featured memorable gold metal performances by Michael Johnson, Amy Van Dyken, Kerri Strug, and Andre Agassi...but you might also remember the tragic bombing that took place in Centennial Olympic Park.

> **At 21, Tiger Woods became the youngest golfer to win the Masters Tournament— and by a record 12 strokes.**

The San Francisco 49ers beat the San Diego Chargers 49–26 at Super Bowl XXIX, setting two new records: highest-scoring Super Bowl and most touchdown passes in a Super Bowl game (six from MVP Steve Young).

But almost certainly, the most memorable sports-related story from this time was the Tonya Harding/Nancy Kerrigan assault. Despite her injuries, inflicted on her by Harding's ex-husband and a metal baton, Kerrigan went on to win the silver medal at the Winter Olympics in Lillehammer.

WHEN YOU
WERE A KID

"I WANT MY
BABY BACK, BABY BACK,
BABY BACK, BABY BACK..."

POP CULTURE

It was a great time to be a kid: you could beg your parents for a Nintendo 64 game system, Tamagotchi virtual pet, Pretty Pretty Princess dress-up game, Laser Challenge Duel Set, Treasure Trolls, Pogs, or, if you *really* wanted to be cool, an oversized Starter jacket.

But let us not forget Beanie Babies! Whether you had the full-sized versions or the diminutive Teenie Beanies found at McDonald's (or both!), no one could get enough of these small stuffed animals with iconic heart-shaped tags on their ears—the most collectible was Princess the Bear, named after Princess Diana.

Commercial jingles were especially memorable: you can probably still recite every word to songs featured in ads for Chili's Baby Back Ribs, Kit Kat Bars, and Meow Mix. (Hint: the first word is "meow"…)

Probably too young to grow "90210" sideburns, you may have asked your hair-cutter to give you a "Curtained Cut" or a "Rachel," depending on which shows and movies you watched.

WHEN YOU
WERE A KID

WHEN YOU WERE A TEENAGER...

IN THE NEWS

The events of September 11th, 2001,
were shocking and difficult for everyone,
but for you especially this day may represent
a loss of childhood innocence. You will likely
always remember where you were when
you heard that the Twin Towers had fallen.

In response to these attacks, the Department of Homeland
Security was formally established to "detect, prepare for,
prevent, protect against, respond to, and recover from
terrorist attacks within the United States."

United States and allies invaded Iraq on suspicion of its
government having weapons of mass destruction. Though
Saddam Hussein was removed from power, the Iraq War
would officially continue for the next nine years, resulting
in countless civilian casualties.

The space shuttle Columbia unexpectedly disintegrated
after its return from a successful 16-day mission. All seven
astronauts were killed, and debris from the shuttle rained
across hundreds of miles of Texas countryside.

WHEN YOU
WERE A TEEN

Your first real education of the electoral process may have begun with the words "hanging chads" and "butterfly ballots." After months of recounts, petitions, and federal appeals, George W. Bush was declared the winner of the 2000 presidential election by a mere 537 votes.

The Human Genome Project—a massive international undertaking—announced that it had finally mapped all known human genes. It was an incredible achievement, given that, if uncoiled, the DNA in all the cells in the human body would extend beyond 10 billion miles.

Massachusetts became the first state in the union to issue marriage licenses to same-sex couples, paving the way for other states to follow suit in the future.

Your late teen years were a bad time for natural disasters: Hurricane Katrina claimed the lives of nearly 2,000 New Orleans natives (and the homes of many, many more), and a massive earthquake measuring 9.0 on the Richter scale loosed a disastrous tsunami on Southeast Asia, killing over 225,000 and displacing 1.2 million more.

WHEN YOU
WERE A TEEN

MUSIC

You once listened to your music on cassette tapes, then CDs...and then it became digital. You may have first heard about MP3s via the file-sharing program Napster, which was sued for copyright infringement. No worries, though—just three years later you were able to make perfectly legal transactions at the iTunes Store.

Teen pop stars Christina Aguilera and Britney Spears "grew up," transitioning from more innocent pop songs "Come On Over Baby (All I Want is You)" and "Oops!... I Did It Again" to more provocative hits like "Dirrty" and "I'm a Slave 4 U," respectively.

American Idol **launched the careers of dozens of performers, including Kelly Clarkson, Carrie Underwood, and Philip Phillips. (As well as musical oddity William Hung.)**

Other hit songs often heard on your CD player or iPod Mini may have included "How You Remind Me" by Nickelback, "Complicated" by Avril Lavigne, and "In da Club" by 50 Cent.

MOVIES

Spider-Man, starring Tobey Maguire and Kirsten Dunst, was the first massively successful superhero movie, and it paved the way for a string of comic book-inspired movies you either anticipated with glee... or tried to ignore.

Peter Jackson's massively epic (and epically massive) *Lord of the Rings* film trilogy was the movie event of the decade, introducing you and your friends to the elfish good looks of Orlando Bloom and the beginning of many, many Gollum impressions.

Aspiring Hogwarts students got to relive Harry, Ron, and Hermione's early adventures on the big screen as Warner Brothers began to release one *Harry Potter* movie each year.

Other memorable hit movies of your teenage years include *The Pianist*, *Seabiscuit*, *The Ring*, *Pirates of the Caribbean: The Curse of the Black Pearl*, *Eternal Sunshine of the Spotless Mind*, *Mean Girls*, and *The Notebook*.

WHEN YOU
WERE A TEEN

TV

Spanning nine seasons and four lead actors, *The X-Files* aired its final episode, but conspiracy fans wouldn't have to wait too long for their next mystery fix: *Lost* premiered two years later, featuring an incredible two-hour-long pilot that cost as much as fourteen million dollars to produce.

Fueled by a craze for teen entertainment, *Dawson's Creek* launched the careers of several young actors, and though wildly popular with teens for dealing with real teen issues, it wasn't as popular with some parents, who criticized the show for being too sexy.

Other popular shows you watched may have included *Everwood, The O.C., Arrested Development, The West Wing, Buffy the Vampire Slayer, The Simple Life,* and *Scrubs.*

WHEN YOU
WERE A TEEN

MEGA-POPULAR "REALITY TV"
SHOWS LIKE *SURVIVOR, THE
OSBOURNES,* AND *THE APPRENTICE*
BEGAN TO ECLIPSE SCRIPTED
DRAMAS AND COMEDIES.

SPORTS

Though his legacy as "the greatest basketball player of all time" was already secure, Michael Jordan came out of retirement once more to play for the Washington Wizards. He promised to donate his salary to a relief fund for the victims of 9/11.

The World Wrestling Federation (WWF), perhaps a staple of your younger years, settles a lawsuit initiated by The World Wildlife Fund by changing its name to World Wrestling Entertainment (WWE). With the acquisition of World Championship Wrestling (WCW) and Extreme Championship Wrestling (ECW), WWE became (by far) the largest wrestling promotion in the world.

The Williams sisters—Venus and Serena—dominated the world of tennis, even facing off against each other in several matches.

Long-beleaguered Boston Red Sox fans had their day when their team beat the St. Louis Cardinals to win their first World Series Championship in eighty-six years. The "Curse of the Bambino" was at last reversed!

WHEN YOU WERE A TEEN

POP CULTURE

You said goodbye to the '90s and hello to the new millennium while toasting age-appropriate, nonalcoholic bubbly (*right?*) as a brand-new ball, inscribed with symbols for "hope," lowered on Times Square.

> **Crocs were in, low-carb diets like Atkins were all the rage, many were abuzz with energy drinks, and, after 9/11, it seemed that everyone had an American flag sticker on their car window or bumper.**

Having thankfully survived the dreaded Y2K bug, computers and the Internet became more important to your evolving social life: chat programs like AOL Instant Messenger and MSN Messenger were likely a large part of your daily conversation with friends, and websites like Livejournal and Myspace offered a unique way to express yourself.

Muggles of all ages made time to read about the Boy Who Lived. J. K. Rowling's endearing books spawned several successful movies and a plethora of merchandise, but they were not loved by all—some schools banned the books for fear that they promoted witchcraft.

WHEN YOU
WERE A TEEN

WHEN YOU WERE IN YOUR 20s...

IN THE NEWS

US Airways Flight 1549 was struck by a flock of geese shortly after takeoff, and Captain Chesley B. "Sully" Sullenberger became a national hero after making a crash landing in the Hudson River. Incredibly, no lives were lost.

An explosion on an oil rig fifty miles off the coast of Louisiana killed eleven workers and eventually resulted in the worst oil spill in U.S. history.

Haiti was hit by a magnitude-7 earthquake, devastating the small Caribbean country and displacing 1.5 million people from their homes.

Iceland's Eyjafjallajökull volcano erupted for the first time since 1821, sending a plume of volcanic ash 30,000 feet into the air and grounding airplanes from the United Kingdom to Russia for six days.

Almost 23 million Americans watched the royal wedding ceremony of Prince William and Kate Middleton, Duchess of Cambridge, at Westminster Abbey in London.

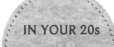

IN YOUR 20s

EVENTS

From humble beginnings to 44th President of the United States, Barack Obama showed the world that the American dream is very much alive.

The "Great Recession," which began with the collapse of AIG, Lehman Brothers, and Bear Sterns, might have made it difficult for you and your friends to find your dream job, house, or apartment.

We learned that there's water on the moon! Or, *in* the moon—though its surface is as dry as any desert on Earth, frozen water beneath the moon's surface could someday be used to support human colonies. It's the stuff of science fiction! Or is it?

President Obama's controversial landmark bill—the Patient Protection and Affordable Care Act—passed in Congress and was signed into law, promising basic health insurance for everyone, regardless of age, sex, or preexisting conditions.

IN YOUR 20s

MUSIC

Online radio streaming services like Pandora, Spotify, or Grooveshark offered anyone the ability to play a personalized selection of music through their computer or smartphone.

The world was stunned to learn that Michael Jackson died of a drug overdose less than a month before his sold-out concerts in London. Grieving fans bought 35 million of his albums, making Jackson the best-selling artist of 2009.

The title track from Lady Antebellum's second album, *Need You Now*, introduced the Nashville trio to those who might not usually listen to country music. They took home both Song of the Year and Album of the Year at the 2011 Grammy Awards.

Popular hit songs you might have played on loop included "Boom Boom Pow" by The Black Eyed Peas, "California Gurls" by Katy Perry (featuring Snoop Dogg), and "Moves like Jagger" by Maroon 5 (featuring Christina Aguilera).

MOVIES

After *Avatar*, suddenly it seemed that every blockbuster movie had a 3D version. Thanks to all the movie-viewing options at your disposal, ticket sales had been declining for years—movie studios struggled to find ways to lure people back to the cinema.

Kathryn Bigelow became the first woman to win Best Director at the Academy Awards for *The Hurt Locker*, which depicted the story of a bomb-disposal team during the Iraq War.

Movie reboots of some familiar franchises capitalized on your '80s and '90s nostalgia (with sometimes-mixed results). Even toys and board games weren't safe: you likely remember *Battleship, G.I. Joe: The Rise of Cobra*, and of course the very successful *Transformers* series...

You may have also seen *The Hangover, Up, The Social Network, Gravity, How to Train Your Dragon, The Help, Star Trek*, or *The Hunger Games*.

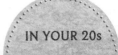

IN YOUR 20s

TV

Thanks to online streaming services like Hulu, Netflix, and Amazon Prime, you may never have to shell out money for an expensive cable package. And even if you do, you don't have to rush home to watch a show when it actually airs, like your parents did, thanks to the magic of "On Demand."

Though certainly not the first to do so, hit shows *Glee* and *Modern Family* were widely praised for featuring openly gay characters in a way that portrayed them as people, not stereotypes.

Other shows you may have watched (or still do!) include *The Office, Breaking Bad, Parks and Recreation, The Big Bang Theory, Friday Night Lights, Community, How I Met Your Mother, Supernatural, 30 Rock, Parenthood,* and *House.*

IN YOUR 20s

Were you on Team COCO? Unhappy with ratings, NBC took the *Tonight Show* away from new host Conan O'Brien and returned the late-night television staple to former host Jay Leno. O'Brien's fans rallied behind him, resulting in a lot of embarrassing headlines for NBC and Leno.

The United States broke the record for the most medals won at a single Winter Olympics in 2010, with Americans Bode Miller and Shaun White having memorable breakout performances.

Tennis fans witnessed the longest match in tennis history as American John Isner played Nicolas Mahut of France at the Wimbledon Championships over the course of three days, for a total of 11 hours and 5 minutes.

American cyclist Lance Armstrong survived cancer to take home seven Tour de France titles—only to have all of them stripped away after allegations of performance-enhancing drug use.

Led by the "Big Three"—LeBron James, Chris Bosh, and Dwyane Wade—the Miami Heat won two NBA Finals against the Oklahoma City Thunder and then the San Antonio Spurs.

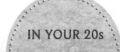

IN YOUR 20s

POP CULTURE

Technology is an intrinsic part of daily life
now—you likely depend on GPS when
you drive (even, sometimes, when you
know the way), your smartphone likely sleeps
next to you, and social media like Facebook
and Twitter can ignite a revolution…
or keep you in touch with your grandma,
depending on how you use it.

The original Nintendo Entertainment System came out
when you were born, and since then video games have
evolved by eye-popping degrees. "Next-generation"
consoles PlayStation 4 and the Xbox One are capable
of graphics you could only dream of when you were
playing *The Oregon Trail* at school or *Donkey Kong 64* on
your N64.

Unlike your parents, who may have been married in
their early 20s, you were more likely to wait until your
mid- to late 20s before taking the plunge.

If you've had children, you were likely to name your
boy(s) Jacob, Mason, Noah, Liam, or Ethan; your girl(s):
Sophia, Emma, Isabella, Olivia, or Ava.

NOW YOU'RE 30!

And you're in good company!
Look who else is in their 30s:

- Michael Phelps, swimmer
- Mark Zuckerberg, Facebook founder
- Beyoncé Knowles, musician
- Ryan Gosling, actor
- Justin Timberlake, musician
- Keira Knighley, actress
- Cristiano Ronaldo, soccer player
- Lily Allen, musician
- LeBron James, basketball player
- Danica Patrick, racecar driver
- Prince William and Prince Harry, British royalty
- Anne Hathaway, actress
- Katy Perry, musician
- T-Pain, musician and producer
- Lindsey Jacobellis, snowboarder
- Bruno Mars, musician

"Thirty was so strange for me. I've really had to come to terms with the fact that I am now a walking and talking adult."

—*C. S. Lewis*

"The boy gathers materials for a temple, and then when he is thirty, concludes to build a woodshed."

—*Henry David Thoreau*

"In my thirties, I felt I had hold of one of the reins some of the time."

—*Chaka Khan*

DID YOU ENJOY THIS BOOK?

We would love to hear from you.

Please send your comments to:
Hallmark Book Feedback
P.O. Box 419034
Mail Drop 100
Kansas City, MO 64141

Or e-mail us at:
booknotes@hallmark.com

This is not the end...!
It's only the beginning!

Every day is another chance
to make something happen —
Well, let it rip!

Love you,
Mom